T0199202

When I Grow Up, I Want to See the World

Kenya Boyd

Print information available on the last page

Rev. date: 04/24/2018

To order additional copies of this book, contact:
Xlibris
1-888-795-4274
www.Xlibris.com
Orders@Xlibris.com

Dedication

Thank you Arlan and Bettina for allowing me to be bit by the travel bug. Much gratitude to my spiritual and emotional supporters for encouraging and reminding me of my gifts and dreams: Brandie, Cheri and Terrance.

He said that it is so huge that it's big enough for seven continents and LOTS of countries.

There are billions of people who I've never even seen before! They look different than me, talk different than me, and do different things. My teacher told us that's called their culture. That means they may live, eat, and celebrate differently than Americans.

Then, I will go to Rio de Janeiro, Brazil! You can find me bird watching in the rainforest or celebrating at a huge festival, called Carnival where everyone wears colorful outfits and dances in celebration of Lent.

I will eat lots of feijoada and stand on top of the world.

I want to see Tokyo, Japan. I can't wait to eat mochi and onigiri in front of Tokyo Tower. Wearing a kimono, I will bow and say 'ohayo gozaimasu' before morning tea in the Emperor's garden.

There are tea houses and places called street markets where people eat all kinds of food and watch shows from the street performers in Taipei, Taiwan. I can drink bubble tea, eat soup dumplings, beef noodles, steamed dumplings, or even fermented veggies.

Ooh, how could I forget! I have to make my wishes at the Fountain of Trevi.

In Seoul, South Korea, I can wear a traditional Hanbok dress on holidays or...

Dress up like the guards who protected the castles from enemies years ago. Such hard work! I bet they ate lots of bibibop to stay strong.

When I go to London, England, I will visit with the Queen. We will have tea and biscuits while we discuss the Royal Family and all the beautiful palaces. It must be hard to be a queen. Fashion is a must!

In Ocho Rios, Jamaica, they eat patties, jerk chicken, mango, and sugar cane. There are adventures around every corner, like: swimming with dolphins, bobsledding, and climbing Dunn's River Falls. And after a long day, you can sit on the beach and sip water from a coconut!!

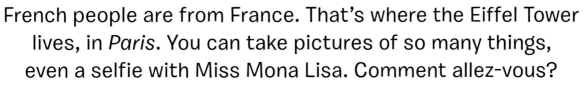

French people are from France. That's where the Eiffel Tower lives, in *Paris*. You can take pictures of so many things, even a selfie with Miss Mona Lisa. Comment allez-vous?

You see! The world is such a big place. I have to get started!
I want to go EVERYWHERE and see Everyone and do everything.
When I grow up, I am going to see the world!

Printed in the United States
By Bookmasters